EXTREME CAREERS

EPIDEMIOLOGISTS

Life Tracking Deadly Diseases

Dana Asher

the rosen publishing group's
rosen central

This book is dedicated to the epidemiologists who devote their lives to making our lives healthier, safer, and better understood.

Published in 2003 by The Rosen Publishing Group, Inc.
29 East 21st Street, New York, NY 10010

Library of Congress Cataloging-in-Publication Data

Asher, Dana.
Epidemiologists : life tracking deadly diseases / Dana Asher— 1st ed.
p. cm. — (Extreme careers)
Summary: Highlights the background and experiences of people who track diseases in large populations and try to discover the causes of those diseases.
Includes bibliographical references and index.
ISBN 0-8239-3633-3 (lib. bdg.)
1. Epidemiology—Juvenile literature. 2. Epidemiology—Vocational guidance—Juvenile literature. 3. Epidemiologists—Juvenile literature. [1. Epidemiology. 2. Epidemiology—Vocational guidance. 3. Vocational guidance.] I. Title. II. Series.
RA653.5 .A845 2002
614.4—dc21

2001008155

Manufactured in the United States of America

Contents

What Is Epidemiology?

Put out that cigarette, your mom tells your grand-mother—they've proven that smoking causes lung cancer. That hamburger is undercooked, your neighbor says, pointing to the patty on your plate at a backyard barbecue—they say that bacteria in raw meat can make you sick. They say that kids who are bullied are more likely to suffer from depression, your school counselor explains during a lecture. But who exactly are "they"? And how do they know all this information?

"We are they," says Dr. Mark Klebanoff, director of the Division of Epidemiology, Statistics and Prevention Research at the National Institutes of Health (NIH) in Bethesda, Maryland, a top medical

Epidemiologists track and study disease, and how it is spread. For example, studies by epidemiologists helped uncover the link between foot-and-mouth disease and unsafe meat. The Argentine beef pictured here is in a processing plant outside of Buenos Aires.

Epidemiologists: Life Tracking Deadly Diseases

research center and the focus for medical research in the United States. "Epidemiologists do the research and we can figure out what causes certain diseases. Then, we work to inform people how to prevent sickness."

Epidemiology is the study of how and why diseases occur in different groups of people. Research is a large part of an epidemiologist's job. Like investigators at the scene of a crime, these disease detectives begin by looking for clues. Why do some people get sick when

Wildlife pathologist Ward B. Stone examine a dead crow for any trace of the West Nile encephalitis virus that caused a health scare in New York City in 1999. Veterinarians from all over the New York region shipped dead crows for him to inspect.

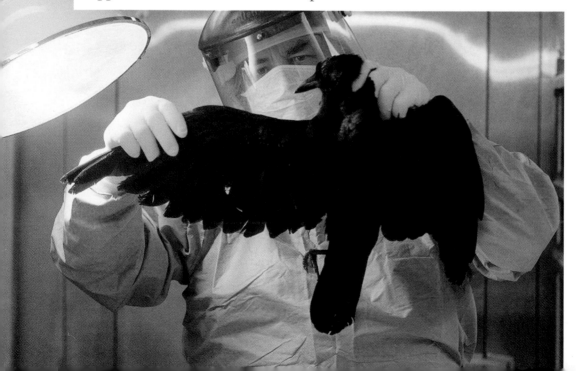

others do not? What makes you more likely to get sunburned than your dark-haired cousin? Why didn't we know about a disease like West Nile virus five years ago, when today neighborhoods are being sprayed with chemicals to prevent the disease (which is often found in birds)? Is there something in our surroundings that makes people develop cancer, or is it a gene hidden in our bodies from the time we are born? If cancer is something found in the environment, will staying far away from its potential source—microwaves, contaminated water, alcohol—prevent the disease?

Determining the answers to these questions takes some thoughtful investigative work. After all, illnesses—whether acute (quick and severe, such as food poisoning or chicken pox) or chronic (continuing for a long time or recurring, such as asthma or diabetes)—leave clues. One discovery leads to another, sort of like putting together a puzzle. When you first begin, there are seventy-five pieces on the floor and you're scratching your head trying to understand their relationship. But if you look at the picture on the box and start with just two pieces that fit, eventually you'll create a sensible picture. As you assemble each section, you gain a better idea of the pieces that fit and those that don't. Disease detectives—epidemiologists—work in much the same way. They begin with the known facts about a disease, and then assemble them together to create a full picture.

Still, there's a major difference between assembling the pieces of a puzzle and figuring out how the clues of a disease fit together. At one time, no one knew why polio put children and young adults into wheelchairs. Today, the illness is nearly eliminated through the vaccinations you get at your doctor's office. Epidemiologists save lives. These medical detectives follow the clues to solve a mystery—or at least attach one more piece of the puzzle. Every time epidemiologists come inches closer to understanding a disease, the public has a better chance of staying healthy.

Milestones in Epidemiology

While high-tech computers and research labs can help epidemiologists stake out a disease today, there will always be a place for what Dr. Mark Klebanoff calls "shoe leather epidemiology." This means that the most effective research may involve simply asking people thoughtful questions. If scientists ask specific questions of those close to someone who is sick, or of the patients themselves, it helps them determine what makes the people who become ill different from those who do not.

Indeed, that is exactly what has helped medical researchers eliminate diseases throughout history. Early epidemiologists asking those very questions—for instance, why is John sick and George well?—have erased some terrible illnesses from the medical books.

Epidemiologists study why disease affects human populations. For example, when the bubonic plague killed a third of Europe's population in the year 1350 (as depicted in this painting *The Plague in Milan* by Casper de Crayer), everyone was baffled as to why it claimed so many lives.

"When there seems to be an increase in illnesses beyond what we would expect, people historically wanted to know why, because if we can learn why a disease happens, we can work on preventing it," says Dr. Klebanoff. When the bubonic plague, or Black Death, as it became known, occurred in 1350, killing more than one-third of Europe's population in just two years, people began to ask why. Was it because the stars were lined up in a particular way? Were they being punished for bad behavior? Today we know that the movement of planets or terrible acts such as stealing or murder don't result in disease or injury. As we understood more about what really caused disease, we began to search for answers in different places.

John Snow and London's Cholera Epidemic

During the 1830s and 1840s, London, the capital of England, had become a filthy city. Animal droppings littered footpaths and slaughterhouses were located on public street corners. Even worse, the waste from houses was channelled underneath them, creating cesspits. This was 160 years ago, before sewer systems had been developed. In 1854, an outbreak of cholera occurred in the city. People experienced severe diarrhea. As a result, they became dehydrated and eventually died.

In one London neighborhood, where Cambridge Street met Broad Street, the number of cholera cases was so great that 500 people died in just ten days. A doctor named John Snow became interested in the case. Snow believed that cholera was a contagious disease caused by a poison in the human body. He wrote an article suggesting that the source of the illness was water that was contaminated with poison. Snow's theory challenged the more common view held by other medical experts of the day, who believed that victims caught the disease by breathing in poisons from the air.

In the midst of a city meeting, Snow announced that water from a public pump was causing many people to get sick and die. He advised that the handle of the water pump on Broad Street be removed. After the local government removed the pump handle, the

In 1854, a serious outbreak of cholera in London, England, prompted Dr. John Snow to theorize that dirty water and sewage were to blame for the spread of the disease.

number of cholera cases decreased and then stopped. This became such an important case in the history of epidemiology that when high-level health officials are faced with complex public-health issues, they ask, "Where is the handle on this Broad Street pump?"

James Lind and Scurvy

While Snow may be one of the most famous epidemiologists, he wasn't the first. In 1747, a surgeon in the English navy named James Lind observed that sailors suffered from a condition called scurvy, which causes swollen and bleeding gums, spots on the skin, and exhaustion.

Often at sea for many months, these sailors did not eat well-rounded, fresh, nutritious meals. As the HMS *Salisbury* sailed from England to the Plymouth Colony, Dr. Lind, the ship's doctor, decided to perform a simple experiment to determine what might be an effective cure for scurvy. He divided twelve sick men into six groups, changing the diets of each group. For example, one drank a quart of apple juice a day, while another received two spoonfuls of vinegar three times a day. As a result, he made a miraculous discovery: The men who received two oranges and one lemon each day recovered immediately. After this experiment, the British navy made sure that sailors received citrus fruits such as limes and lemons for their voyages—and that's why English sailors are sometimes called "limeys."

This drawing depicts ship doctor James Lind, who distributed citrus fruits to British sailors on the HMS *Salisbury*, which helped wipe out the scurvy that had been afflicting British seamen during transatlantic voyages in the early eighteenth century.

Similarly, Dr. Joseph Goldberger did research and discovered what other vitamins—or the lack of them—can do to the body. During the early 1900s, pellagra, a disease that is caused by a diet lacking in vitamin B, killed many poor southerners. People afflicted with the condition had changes in the skin, severe nerve dysfunction, mental disorders, and diarrhea. Even though most doctors believed differently, Dr. Goldberger, a physician in the U.S. government's hygenic laboratory, conducted a series of research experiments. His tests showed that it was nutrients missing from the people's diets and not germs that caused the condition. He warned Americans about the important link between poor nutrition and pellagra.

To definitively prove his point, on April 26, 1916, Dr. Goldberger injected the blood of somebody suffering from pellagra into the arm of his assistant, and then his assistant injected the same into him. The researchers even wiped their noses with tissues used by people already sick with the disease, a certain route to illness if, in fact, pellagra was caused by germs. When they remained healthy, they seemed to have proved their argument that the condition most certainly wasn't caused by germs at all.

Sir Richard Doll, Sir Austin Bradford Hill, and Lung Cancer

While it was quite rare prior to the 1930s and 1940s, lung cancer became more and more common in the years immediately following World War II. This prompted two English epidemiologists, Sir Richard Doll and Sir Austin Bradford Hill, to do a study comparing people who developed lung cancer with those who did not. At first, they thought that it had something to do with road tar. They asked all sorts of questions, including, almost as an afterthought, if the people in the study smoked cigarettes. They found that those who smoked were ten times more likely to get lung cancer than those who didn't.

On September 30, 1950, the *British Medical Journal* published the important results of their research in a paper titled "Smoking and Carcinoma of the Lung," which provided clear evidence of the dangers of ciga-rette smoking. Since then, there have been tens of thousands of papers confirming that smoking causes lung cancer, as well as many other cancers and

In January 1964, U.S. Surgeon General Luther Terry, pictured here holding up a copy of his office's report on lung cancer, declared that smoking had been pinpointed as a direct cause of cancer.

conditions, including heart disease and emphysema. By 1964, the United States surgeon general officially announced that smoking causes cancer.

While today's diseases may be different and, in some cases, the scientific tools more advanced, often the work of an epidemiologist is the same as it has been throughout the centuries. Whether it involves removing the handle from the Broad Street pump, adding citrus fruits to the diets of sailors at sea, or determining that smoking increases the chances of developing lung cancer, one thing remains the same. Somewhere, we have an epidemiologist to thank for the discovery. And by solving a medical mystery, we can work to prevent it in generations to come.

A Degree
of Curiosity

If you've decided that medical detective work sounds fascinating, working as an epidemiologist might be the career to strive for in the future. But if you're like most people who choose to become epidemiologists, your future won't be quite as clear-cut as attending a four-year college and then heading to medical school. While it is possible to become an epidemiologist in this way, for most future medical detectives it doesn't happen like that at all.

There is no single career path to becoming an epidemiologist. To become a practicing lawyer, you have to finish law school and pass the bar exam. To work as a certified public accountant you have to study accounting and pass the CPA exam. But

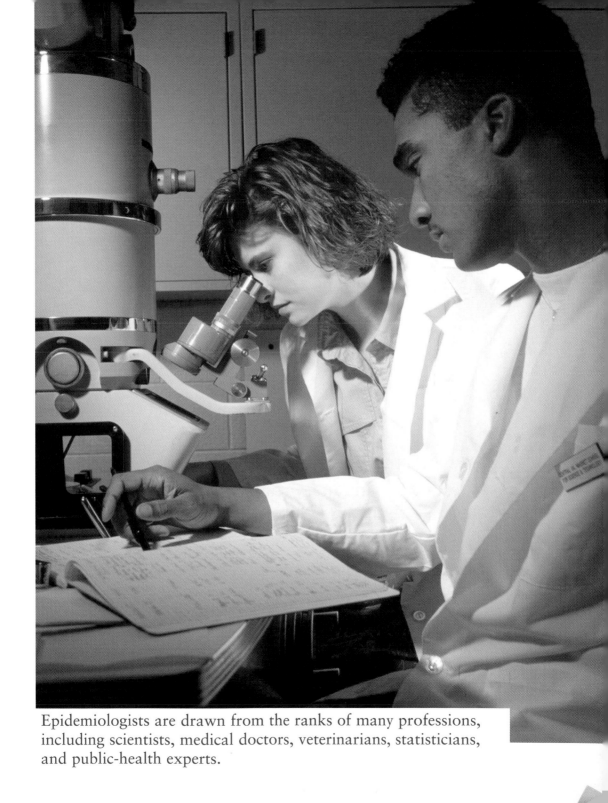

Epidemiologists are drawn from the ranks of many professions, including scientists, medical doctors, veterinarians, statisticians, and public-health experts.

epidemiologists come from many different fields. Some have medical degrees while others have been trained as different types of health-care professionals, such as veterinarians, dentists, laboratory scientists, statisticians, and other public-health professionals.

Searching for a Missing Link

More than anything, "you need curiosity" to succeed as an epidemiologist, according to Dr. Klebanoff of the NIH. "You need a willingness to question what everybody thinks is true. This is true in any research field. You don't need to be a mathematician. You need to be comfortable with math but you don't necessarily have to be very, very good at it."

Let's say that you're intrigued by this talk of becoming a medical detective. You enjoy figuring things out and are really interested in medicine, the human body, and understanding disease. Certainly one of the best places to start learning is by studying biology (the study of life in all its forms and process-es) and medicine, which offers an advanced take on

A biology teacher goes over facts in a textbook with a student. For those seeking to become epidemiologists, studying biology can serve as an important first step in training how to track and explain the progression of disease.

biology and the inner workings of the human body. Studying medicine prepares prospective physicians to diagnose and treat diseases in individuals.

But wait, you say, doesn't that sound a lot like epidemiology? Aren't all doctors, by virtue of what they do, epidemiologists? Both health-care practitioners and epidemiologists observe diseases or conditions, and create hypotheses (educated assumptions or theories) about what causes them, before they try to find a cure. But while a doctor

Students listen to a bioscience lecture at the University of Massachusetts Medical School in Worcester, Massachusetts, in October 2001.

will collect information about an individual patient by taking his or her medical history and conducting a physical exam, epidemiologists collect data about an entire population, or group of people. For example, a doctor will try to determine why a person is suffering from terrible headaches and work to determine what actions to take in order to improve the patient's health. The epidemiologist will try to see why seventeen people in one town are all suffering from similar headaches and what common thread links them together. While the training acquired in medical school will certainly give both traditional doctors and epidemiologists a strong background in science, epidemiologists need additional skills and tactics.

For example, all epidemiologists need to know how to gather information from afflicted populations. If the seventeen headache sufferers live within a half mile of one another, what else do they have in common? Do they all live in a polluted area? Are they all of the same ethnic group, age, or gender? The epidemiologist may notice that all of these people also suffer from other symptoms, such as

Colleges and Universities

Below is a partial list of some of the colleges and universities in the United States that offer degree programs in the field of epidemiology:

Brown University

Colorado State University

Cornell University

Emory University

Harvard University

Loma Linda University

Louisiana State University

Stanford University

Tulane University

University of Arizona

University of California, Berkeley

University of California, Davis

University of California, Irvine

University of California, Los Angeles

University of Colorado

University of Iowa

University of Minnesota

University of Oklahoma

University of Texas, Houston

University of Washington

This is the impressive exterior of Harvard Medical School in Cambridge, Massachusetts, one of the top educational institutions for medicine and biological sciences in the United States.

nasal congestion. Often a headache with congestion is a sign of hay fever. Is it springtime? Does the neighborhood have a large field that produces pollen—the powdery grains from flowers that can make these symptoms appear? By asking all of these questions, the epidemiologist may develop a hypothesis that all seventeen people most likely suffer from hay fever.

But a theory is just that until it's tested—and proven. Perhaps an epidemiologist will send all of the suspected hay fever sufferers to an allergist, who will use more advanced tests to see if they are all allergic to pollen. If the epidemiologist's hypothesis is correct, he or she can prescribe an antihistamine to the sufferers that will relieve some of the symptoms. If not—if he or she finds that only three or four suffer from hay fever and the rest haven't reached for a tissue in weeks, for example—then it's back to the drawing board. With more questions, the epidemiologist might learn that the sufferers all had colds only two weeks before, and sometimes colds turn into sinus infections. In that case, antibiotics might be the cure.

The Importance of Statistics

More than a background in gathering information is required for a career as an epidemiologist, however. Since they are dealing with populations, a big part of their job is to count things—cases of disease or injury and rates of illness, for instance. Another part of the job is to compare those rates with others found in different populations and, through these numbers—called statistics—try to determine patterns. This is how it was discovered that the rates of skin cancer are higher in people who were sunbathers during their youth. Because these people experienced many sunburns, the likelihood of them later developing cancer increased dramatically. They also found that people with fairer skin and hair tend to be more at risk. This data is used to determine the cause of the health problem, the way it is acquired or transmitted, and factors that are related to how at risk someone is for exposure or illness.

More directly, as the field of epidemiology grows in scope and interest, more and more universities are offering programs that help people develop the

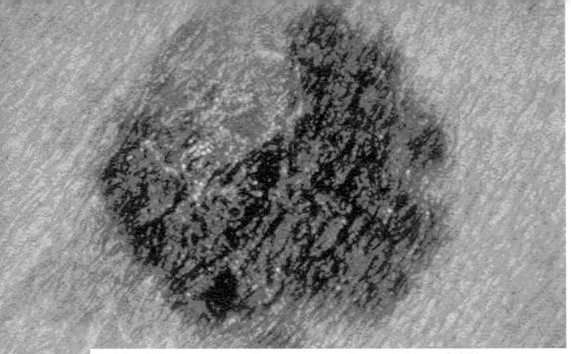

Epidemiologists must often compare the activities of different groups of people to discover the root causes of disease, such as with melanoma (a deadly skin cancer pictured here), which scientists deduced had something to due with overexposure to sunlight.

specific background and knowledge needed for the field. Different areas of epidemiology require different kinds of understanding. Some require hematology (the study of blood), urinalyses (analyzing urine), chemistry, microbiology (the branch of biology dealing with microscopic organisms), immunology (the study of the immune system), and others.

Some colleges and universities now offer courses and degree programs in epidemiology. Harvard's Department of Epidemiology not only teaches the epidemiology of cancer, heart disease, and other illnesses, but does research as well. But you don't have to be in a university's medical school to study epidemiology. For example, Harvard's Department of Nutrition also provides training and research opportunities relating to nutrition and how it affects public health. Questions of how what you eat puts you at risk for diabetes are addressed here, as are questions of how being overweight increases your chances of getting cancer.

At the University of Pennsylvania, you don't have to be working toward a Doctor of Medicine (M.D.) degree to study epidemiology. The Center for Clinical Epidemiology and Biostatistics, the Department of Biostatistics and Epidemiology, and the Graduate Group in Epidemiology and Biostatistics all offer a wide range of courses for medical and other students in master's degree and Doctor of Philosophy (Ph.D.) programs. By taking these courses, students learn how to conduct research on groups of people and how to interpret statistics.

Other agencies even offer on-the-job training. Every year, the Centers for Disease Control and

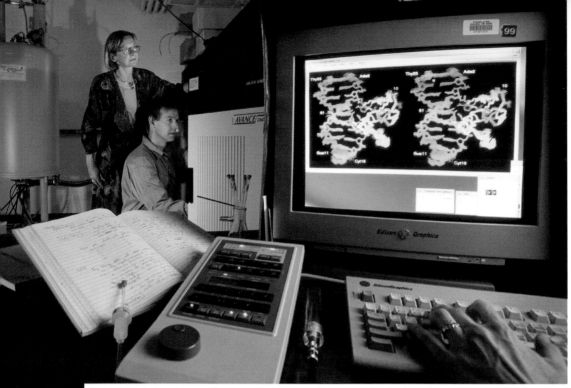

Epidemiologists of all stripes can be greatly helped in their jobs by employing the latest technological advances, such as the computer models these scientists use to study molecules.

Prevention's Epidemiology Program Office selects between sixty and eighty people from among the United States's top health professionals to enter the Epidemic Intelligence Service (EIS) and learn skills essential to maintaining public health.

The last skill required if you have an interest in the field of epidemiology is stamina. Epidemiology is difficult, intense work, and research often leads you down the wrong path before discovering the true solution to your mystery, which is the right cure for a particular illness or condition. It is a career that can be as frustrating as it is illuminating. But if you are a person who loves a challenge and can handle complex reasoning and problem solving, you might just be considering the right field.

An Epidemic of Jobs

The job of a medical super sleuth will never go out of style. After all, there will always be new diseases and new environments for them. When you consider that such diseases can also mutate (transform into a different form) and sometimes resist previous treatments, there will always be a need for people to discover the source of illness. Unlike water carriers, who had to find a new job once plumbing started bringing water into homes, and horse-and-buggy drivers, who had to find different work once automobiles took over the road, epidemiologists will always be needed. They'll just have new and different tools to do their jobs.

The research and work of epidemiologists can have a wide-ranging impact on international health issues, such as this vote in the United Nations Security Council to intensify AIDS education efforts.

Moreover, there are specialties within the field of epidemiology. There are experts at observation, who recognize that there is a problem within a widespread group. There are others who gather a group of people with a certain condition and compare their overall condition with that of a healthy group to determine similarities and differences. There are also experts in mathematics who understand how to use statistics to determine the rates of different illnesses. In other cases, there are experts in particular fields who take the epidemiological track within that area. You will find epidemiologists in specialty fields such as environmental studies, nutrition, aging, pediatrics, and so on.

When you consider the job at hand—determining what causes an illness and trying to figure out how to prevent it—it makes sense that all sorts of government agencies, universities, hospitals, and private companies would be interested in having epidemiologists as staff employees. After all, it's a career that is much more than just figuring out how to make a vaccine so fourth graders don't have to miss school due to chicken pox. It's about learning whether the weed killer your dad uses in your backyard garden is safe if you're tossing around a football in the same area, or whether soldiers in the United States Army will get sick with a strange affliction if they go to fight a war in a foreign country.

Think about it: Diseases you've never heard of, like anthrax, suddenly make the front page of your local newspaper. In today's global economy, countries all over the world do business together. The frequency of air travel means that diseases can "fly" to other parts of the world in a matter of hours, as was the case with Ebola that originated in Africa but made its way to other countries, including the United States. Who would have thought that a naturally occurring mineral called asbestos, once used widely in the construction industry, could be found to cause lung problems later? And in the wake of new wars, there have even been concerns about chemicals and diseases brought to the United States on purpose by people who view them as potential weapons more powerful than guns or tanks. In short, epidemiologists work wherever there is a need for medical detectives to determine how diseases, nutrition, environmental factors, or conditions affect public health.

National Government Agencies

The United States government maintains organizations and centers that oversee health concerns for the entire country. The National Institutes of Health (NIH), the workplace of Dr. Mark Klebanoff, has many epidemiologists researching everything from cancer to weight problems. The NIH, which is actually about twenty-five separate institutes and centers, works to uncover new knowledge that will lead to better health for everyone. This involves investigation done in its own labs as well as supporting the research of other scientists in universities, medical schools, hospitals, and research centers all over the world. One of the NIH's most important responsibilities is to spread health information, both to the medical community and the public.

The NIH makes huge contributions to public health. Within the last twenty-five years, the NIH has played a major role in making many achievements possible, including a drop in the mortality (death) rate caused by heart disease, the nation's number-one killer, and a significant increase in the survival rate for cancer patients.

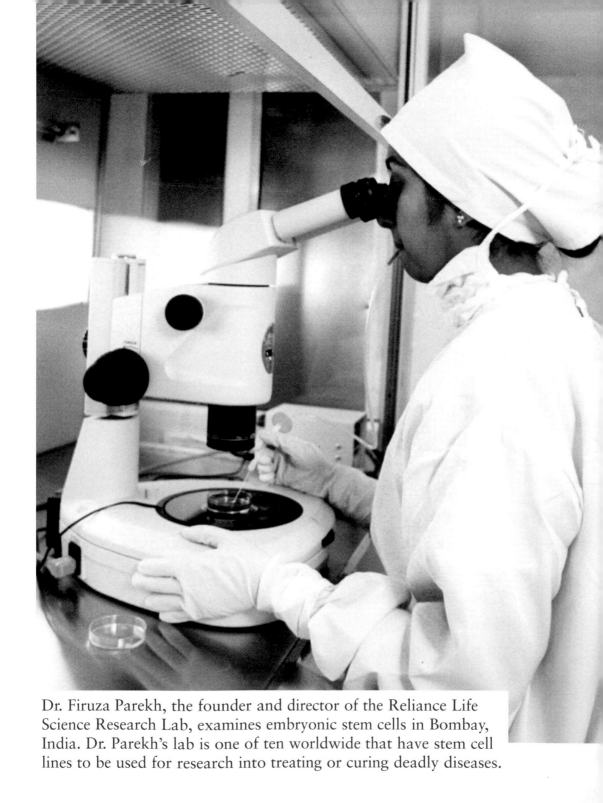

Dr. Firuza Parekh, the founder and director of the Reliance Life Science Research Lab, examines embryonic stem cells in Bombay, India. Dr. Parekh's lab is one of ten worldwide that have stem cell lines to be used for research into treating or curing deadly diseases.

Located in Bethesda, Maryland, just outside Washington, D.C., the NIH is responsible for other important advances over the last few years. For example, rates of paralysis from spinal cord injuries have been reduced by new, rapid procedures, and new treatments have been developed to control everything from depression to schizophrenia. Death rates from stroke were cut in half during the same time. And with better treatments and earlier detection, people have more of a chance of surviving major health problems and diseases than ever before. Moreover, vaccines protect against infectious diseases (diseases that one person can catch from another, like tuberculosis) that once killed and disabled millions of children and adults.

The Centers for Disease Control (CDC) is recognized as the number-one agency for protecting the health and safety of people at home and abroad, and providing up-to-date information to help people make better health choices. This center, based in Atlanta, Georgia, investigates outbreaks of disease domestically and internationally. CDC representatives travel at a moment's notice to investigate outbreaks of disease all over the world. The CDC also investigates food-borne illnesses such as E. coli poisoning, and even works to improve worker safety and health.

The United States also maintains hundreds of agencies and organizations, many of which have epidemiologists on staff even if health isn't the agency's main mission. The U.S. military, which protects our country during times of danger and war, has specialists who work to prevent outbreaks of disease within the armed forces. Whether it's making sure soldiers don't catch diseases during operations abroad or preventing bacterial illnesses from being brought to this country as a result of a foreign military attack, epidemiologists within our military are charged with the medical safety of our armed forces. How can the U.S. Marines protect its personnel against deadly chemicals sprayed in the air? How can we detect dangerous biological agents introduced by our enemies? Epidemiologists are hard at work in these areas.

The Environmental Protection Agency (EPA) has epidemiologists to determine at what level asbestos in the air is dangerous, what makes drinking water safe or unsafe, and what conditions in an office may make workers sick. Even the U.S. Department of

Energy (DOE) has a Comprehensive Epidemiologic Data Resource (CEDR).

State Health Departments

While the NIH and CDC are federal government agencies (that is, they oversee health issues across the country), every state government also has a health department that examines health issues in that particular state. For example, if there is an outbreak of hepatitis in New York, epidemiologists working within that state might explore what the people who are infected have in common to help track the source of the illness. California's Department of Health Services, for instance, offers tips on how to help protect children from lice, while Oklahoma's State Department of Health maintains an Office of Tobacco Use Prevention.

Universities and Colleges

Major universities, particularly those with medical schools, often have epidemiologists that are involved with research on all sorts of health issues. Usually,

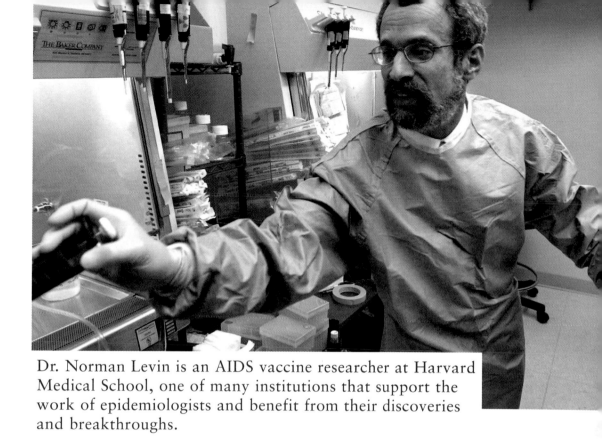

Dr. Norman Levin is an AIDS vaccine researcher at Harvard Medical School, one of many institutions that support the work of epidemiologists and benefit from their discoveries and breakthroughs.

these researchers also teach students at the university. The schools have the funds to help the epidemiologist in his or her study, and the university, in turn, gets a great deal of recognition for having an accomplished researcher on its staff who may, one day, make an important finding. For example, Harvard's Department of Epidemiology is currently researching the role of viruses in cancer. The University of Maryland has epidemiologists on staff who conduct research on everything from women's health to tropical medicine.

Private Institutions

Let's say a big pharmaceutical company is developing a new drug that can help people with asthma just as they are about to have an attack. In addition to being a wonderful medical discovery, it's also a great business opportunity because there are thousands of people with asthma in the United States—and more in other countries—who would love to make use of this type of medicine.

As with any new drug under development, however, years of testing need to be done before any medicine can attain approval from the U.S. Food and Drug Administration (FDA). Mandatory testing is conducted to be certain that the drug works efficiently. Studies are also done to ensure that there are no serious side effects from the medication such as dizziness or heart problems, and even to determine if the drug's benefits outweigh its risks. (For example, some people might be willing to experience a little dizziness if it means they can breathe more easily.) Epidemiologists can help resolve this and many other important questions.

Environmental companies also play a part in the potential work of epidemiologists. For example, say that Paint Brush, Inc., a large (fictitious) company that manufactures paint and sells it worldwide, has a brilliant idea. It's going to make a paint that dries in only five minutes, like nail polish. Even better, only one coat of paint is needed to complete a whole room. To make this special type of paint, however, a new ingredient must be used that has never been tried before. How can Paint Brush, Inc. determine if the new ingredient is safe? How can they be certain that this new element won't cause health problems in the people who use it? After all, lead paint was used for years until it was discovered that children ingesting lead paint chips suffered from health problems like delayed development.

Whether it's a position with a huge company or a post with a government agency, you'll find epidemiology jobs in many different industries. Whether your interest lies in health, nutrition, the environment, or big business, you can no doubt find epidemiological roles within those areas. After all, the more that diseases develop and change, and the study of them advances, the need for savvy epidemiologists will also increase.

Disease Detectives at Work

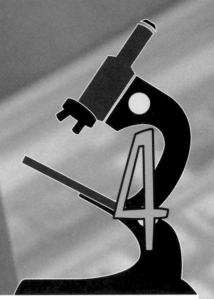

4

What role can epidemiologists play during wartime? They don't drive tanks, plan military operations, or man submarines. But like the Central Intelligence Agency (CIA), they can follow the clues our enemies leave in order to stop biological attacks against people and countries. Biological warfare is when someone uses diseases as weapons, for example, releasing bacteria strains that cause smallpox or anthrax into the environment.

Looking for Clues

At the onset of the war against terrorism in autumn of 2001, anthrax was unleashed in the United States

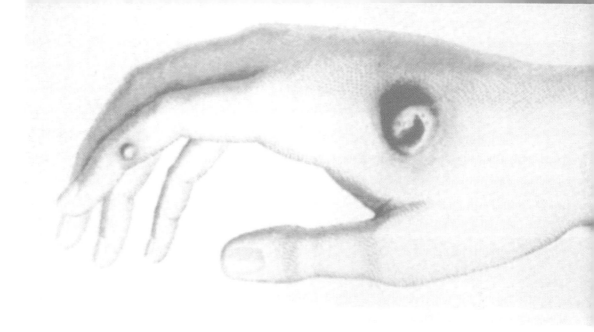

Plate 6.9. Accidental cowpox lesions on the hand of Sarah Nelmes (case XVI in [which material was taken for the vaccination of James Phipps in 1796.

A presentation at the Centers for Disease Control's Smallpox Response and Preparedness Training for States seminar. The CDC looks into disease outbreaks both in the United States and abroad.

against its people. It was the epidemiologists—especially those at the CDC—who were on the front lines, working to understand the mystery of how this rare disease could be purposely used against both individuals and countries. After all, this wasn't anything the United States had ever experienced before, and for epidemiologists it was a new challenge.

On October 4, 2001, Florida doctors determined that a sixty-three-year-old man named Robert Stevens was sick with a deadly form of anthrax called inhalation anthrax, in which one breathes in anthrax particles. Stevens died the next day. The Florida State Department of Health and the CDC were quickly sent to begin an investigation.

Anthrax's incubation period—the time between exposure to the disease and the appearance of its first noticeable symptoms—is usually somewhere between one and seven days, but may be as long as sixty days. The epidemiologists worked to reconstruct Stevens's schedule for the last few weeks of his life to determine where he may have been exposed. They collected samples from objects and the air, and even dust from his home, workplace, and other areas he had visited. They spoke with Stevens's family, coworkers, and doctors.

The CDC even dispatched investigators to North Carolina, where Stevens had been visiting his daughter shortly before he died. Finally, through conversations and lab testing, they determined that there were anthrax spores on his computer keyboard at work.

In addition to figuring out how Stevens became ill, epidemiologists were concerned with preventing others from getting the disease. CDC and state health officials alerted health-care providers to look for unusual cases of respiratory disease, which causes problems with normal breathing. Although anthrax begins with flulike symptoms, it quickly becomes a more serious illness, similar to pneumonia and meningitis. After determining that the bacterium was present at American Media, Inc., the company where Stevens worked, the CDC began testing other employees. A nasal sample (a test taken by rubbing a cotton swab in a patient's nose) of another worker in the building suggested exposure as well. As a preventive measure, public-health officials began to contact employees who had worked in the building since August 1, 2001, to pro-vide necessary antibiotics. If taken before symptoms occur, antibiotics can easily prevent anthrax.

Federal workers carefully clean up the offices of American Media, Inc., in Boca Raton, Florida, in October 2001 after it was discovered that anthrax spores caused the death of one worker and the illness of another.

Since anthrax is not contagious from one person to another, there wasn't a widespread epidemic within American Media, Inc., or the other companies where employees would later show symptoms. But because it can be so deadly, determining how people were exposed was crucial. After examining all the clues and putting the pieces of the puzzle together, epidemiologists determined that Stevens—and the others who had became ill—had been exposed to anthrax through the mail. The next step was for Federal Bureau of

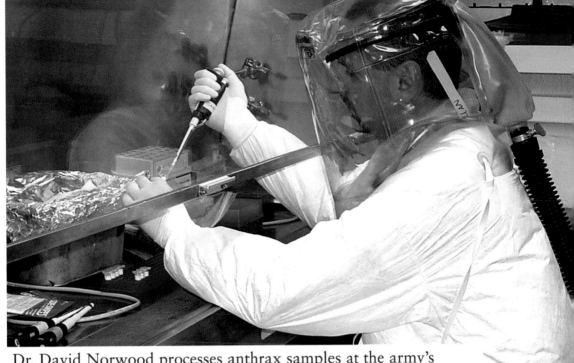

Dr. David Norwood processes anthrax samples at the army's biodefense laboratory in Fort Detrick, Maryland. An anthrax-laced letter was sent to Senator Patrick Leahy in December 2001 and was then turned over to the lab for investigation.

Investigation (FBI) agents and other law enforcement officials to discover who put anthrax in the mail, and how they could stop it from happening again.

The Future

Like many fields, epidemiology advances as developments in science and technology progress. At one time, epidemiologists added numbers without calculators and tried to figure out what caused disease without microscopes or blood tests. As in London in the 1840s, they simply determined that it was bad water that caused cholera and removed the handle from the Broad Street pump. Determining whether more teenage girls in Australia, the United States, or Japan have eating disorders would be more difficult without telephones to speak with other scientists, planes to fly to other countries to conduct studies, or the Internet to help do research and compare studies.

Mathematics is getting more complicated, too, as one discovery leads to another. "As computers get more and more powerful—and as more people can afford to have a powerful computer sitting on their desks—math becomes a new field," says Dr. Klebanoff. Often, these high-tech tools can make doing investigative work much, much easier. But sometimes it makes things even more complicated, as when an answer leads only to another question.

Today, molecular researchers study the smallest units—sometimes just one or two cells, or even the parts of only one cell. A field called genetics studies genes, or the tiny elements of heredity. Genes are a human roadmap, determining everything from a person's height to his or her risk for developing heart disease. As epidemiologists work more closely with these scientists, they understand that the reason Mary is likely to get breast cancer isn't just because her mom and grandmother had the disease. They can actually test her genes and determine whether she has a mutation (alteration) of a particular gene that puts her at risk for breast cancer. Afterward, doctors can counsel her on what to do about it and target areas of her health that could be improved upon in light of the new information.

Molecular biologists, like the scientist pictured here, investigate the tiniest elements of life to help further our understanding of how both genetic background and outside factors contribute to the diseases we suffer as humans.

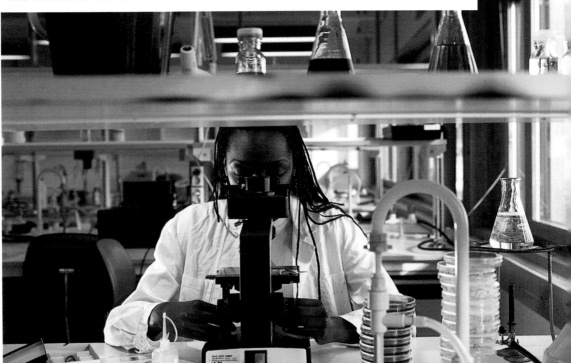

Epidemiologists: Life Tracking Deadly Diseases

Who knows where the future of science will take us? Just twenty-five years ago, we never would have imagined our current success at mapping out human genes, cloning animals, or "smart" drugs that bind to specific receptors or block particular proteins. Chances are, the future of medicine is bright indeed, especially in fields like epidemiology. Perhaps we'll be able to swallow a tiny camera that travels around the body on the lookout for illnesses before they begin. Or maybe we'll be carrying around mini computers that let us know when we are infected with a disease so doctors can treat it before symptoms occur. Maybe we'll even find a cure for colds!

Whatever advances medical science brings, there is one thing that will continue to be the most important tool in epidemiology: a curious mind. Despite the tools scientists and doctors have, a mind that asks questions—and then asks some more—will be the most meaningful instrument humankind has to help solve the mysteries of illness. And that mind may very well be yours.

Glossary

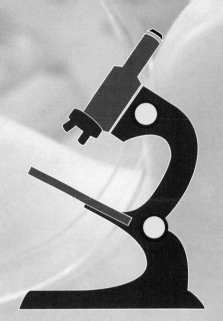

acute Illness or condition that is brief and severe.

antibiotic A medication that causes bacteria to stop growing and die.

asthma An allergic disorder of the respiratory system that causes wheezing and difficulty breathing.

Black Death The bubonic plague, which in 1350 killed more than one-third of Europe's population in only two years.

chicken pox A disease produced by a virus that causes fever and blisters.

cholera A contagious infection that causes severe diarrhea and dehydration.

chronic Illness or condition that is recurring or continues for a long time.

Epidemiologists: Life Tracking Deadly Diseases

contaminated Made unfit for use by the introduction of unwholesome or undesirable elements.

dehydration An abnormal loss of water.

diabetes A blood disorder of high levels of glucose (or sugar).

dysfunction Impaired or abnormal functioning.

epidemic The occurrence of more cases of disease than would normally be expected over a given period of time.

epidemiology The branch of medicine dealing with disease in groups of people, or populations.

federal Pertaining to an entire country.

food poisoning An illness caused by eating food contaminated with bacteria.

hepatitis Swelling of the liver caused by a virus or toxin.

heredity The passing on of genetic traits from parents to children.

immunity A condition in which a host is not susceptible to infection or disease.

infected When a person or animal has a disease.

infection The presence of a parasite or bacteria within a host that may or may not cause disease.

infectious diseases Diseases that can be passed from person to person.

pellagra A disease marked by dermatitis, gastrointestinal disorders, and central nervous symptoms, and associated with a diet deficient in niacin and protein.

population A group of people or things.

risk factor The behavior or lifestyle that makes it more likely that a disease will develop.

scurvy A disease that causes swollen and bleeding gums, spots on the skin, and exhaustion due to a lack of vitamin C.

tuberculosis An infectious disease that affects the lungs.

vaccine A virus or bacterium that has been weakened or killed and that is introduced into the body to create an immunity to it.

For More Information

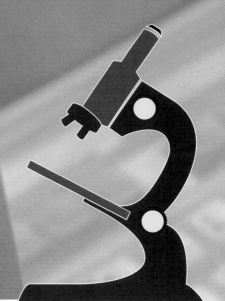

Centers for Disease Control (CDC)
1600 Clifton Road
Atlanta, GA 30333
(800) 311-3435
Web site: http://www.cdc.gov

National Institutes of Health (NIH)
U.S. Department of Health and Human Services
9000 Rockville Pike
Building 31, Room 2B03
Bethesda, MD 20892
(301) 496-4143
Web site: http://www.nih.gov

World Health Organization (WHO)
525 23rd Street NW
Washington, DC 20037
(202) 974-3000
Web site: http://www.who.int

In Canada

Health Canada
Tunney's Pasture
Ottawa, ON K1A OL2
(613) 957-0322
Web site: http://www.hc-sc.gc.ca

Web Sites

Due to the changing nature of Internet links, the Rosen Publishing Group, Inc., has developed an online list of Web sites related to the subject of this book. This site is updated regularly. Please use this link to access the list:

http://www.rosenlinks.com/eca/epid/

For Further Reading

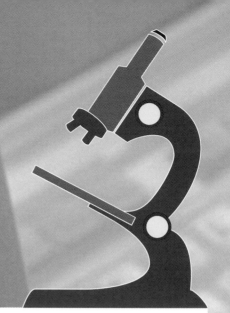

Friedlander, Mark P., and Leonard T. Kurland. *Outbreak: Disease Detectives at Work*. Minneapolis, MN: Lerner Publications Company, 2000.

Powell, Jillian. *World Health Organizations* (World Organizations). New York: Franklin Watts, 2000.

Pringle, Laurence. *Chemical and Biological Weapons: The Cruelest Weapons*, rev. ed. Springfield, NJ: Enslow Publishers, 2000.

Smith, Carter. *Mapping Epidemics: A Historical Atlas of Disease*. New York: Franklin Watts, Inc. 2000.

Yount, Lisa. *Disease Detectives (History Makers)*. San Diego, CA: Lucent Books, 2001.

Bibliography

Goldberger, Joseph. "Goldberger and the 'Pellagra Germ.'" National Institutes of Health, 1996.

Huskey, Robert J., ed. "A Simple Experiment on Scurvy." September 1998. Retrieved September 2001 (http://www.people.virginia.edu/~rjhqu/scurvy1.htm).

Ludwig, Jessica. "UCLA Epidemiologist Creates a Web Site About a Pioneer in the Field." *UCLA Magazine*, No. 12, Summer 2000.

Wynder, Ernst L., and Evarts Graham. "Tobacco Smoking as a Possible Etiologic Factor in Bronchiogenic Carcinoma: A Study of 684 Proven Cases." *Journal of the American Medical Association*, 1950.

Index

About the Author

Dana Asher is a writer and editor living in New Rochelle, New York. She has written extensively on career-related subjects for magazines and Web sites.

Photo Credits

Cover, pp. 5, 6, 18, 24, 30, 39, 43, 47, 50, 51 © AP/Wide World Photos; pp. 10, 15, 21, 32, 35 © Corbis; p. 13 © Hulton/Archive/Getty Images; pp. 23, 27, 53 © Index Stock.

Design

Les Kanturek

Layout

Nelson Sá

Editor

Joann Jovinelly